MW00916621

CONTENTS

The Retail Leader's Field Guide

How to Run a Kick-Ass Store Where Everyone Wants to Work

Kit Campoy

Edited by: Alicia Rust

WELCOME
HELLO

The Retail   Kit Campoy
Leader's
Field Guide:

HOW TO RUN A
KICK-ASS STORE
WHERE EVERYONE
WANTS TO WORK

Included in this book:

Thank You For Reading

(Pg. Numbers eliminated due
to formatting across
various platforms.)

Review This Book on Amazon
Have a Nice Day

PREFACE

Hi, I'm so stoked you're here!

I wrote this book for leaders in the field. So often, leadership advice is written from a CEO perspective and doesn't always relate to the needs of a brick-and-mortar, customer-facing environment.

When you get promoted to a store manager position, everyone expects you to have all the answers, but you don't. The resources provided to you may be slim. This book will help you bridge that resource gap and set you up for success.

Although this book is written for newly promoted store leaders, the advice found here will help leaders at all levels.

Let's dig in.

INTRODUCTION

I was bleary-eyed. It had been a long week on the sales floor. The California sun streamed through the ten-foot windows which wrapped around the building, but the light did little to recharge my overworked body.

Everything hurt, and I was exhausted. I'd been working a mix of open and closing shifts, had helped in shipment, and the customer traffic had been heavy. This morning I opened, ran the floor, helped the cashiers, and stocked the shoe room. I was the only manager in the building until one o'clock.

I'd been watching the time all morning, aching for a break. By 12:30, I couldn't wait to go to lunch and sit down. I was tired, hungry, and thirsty. The minutes ticked by until my closing manager came in.

Finally, she arrived.

The 30-Minute Lunch Break
We chatted, I got her caught up, and I sprinted out the door to get food. Often in retail, you have thirty minutes for a lunch break, so you need to move quickly if you need to buy lunch. On a typical day I'd

return to the store and only have ten minutes to eat.

I arrived back, sat at the management desk, and shut the office door, something I rarely did. But today, I was craving just a small slice of silence. I took a deep breath and a sip of water and unpacked my lunch. Then a knock came at the office door, rapid and urgent. I looked up at the doorknob and reluctantly leaned over to open it. Maybe it was the closing manager looking for her keys. I pulled the door open and saw my opening associate standing there. I was confused; his shift ended thirty minutes ago.

"Hey, man, what's up?" I asked. I had to tilt my head way back to look up at him. He was tall and thin. A black T-shirt hung off his skinny frame. His hands were covered in tattoos. He stepped halfway into the office, keeping the door ajar with his body.

He launched into a story about how his dad died in a car accident, and he was trying to figure out what to do next. He was in his mid-twenties but alone in this somewhat unfamiliar state—he'd recently moved here. He spoke quickly with a heavy Southern drawl, so I had to listen closely. I was trying to put the pieces together.

"Did this just happen? When? When did you find out? How?" I asked.

He spoke a mile-a-minute. He rambled without punctuation, a stream of consciousness.

I stood up, grabbed an extra chair for him and kicked

the door closed. I pushed my lunch aside, as well as my exhaustion. I listened. I gave him space. I answered any questions I could. I didn't look at my watch once. Time no longer mattered. Neither did my food or the sales floor. Everything else faded like a fog had rolled in and nestled around us. At that moment, he was the only person in my life.

Leading Is A Privilege

I can't tell you how honored I am that he came to talk to me that day. It means he felt safe in my presence and trusted me. I only told one other leader because I knew she'd keep it confidential. I needed another leader in the building to understand his situation.

This wasn't the first time I sat in the office with a team member, listening closely to a massive life upheaval, and it wouldn't be the last. Sometimes as leaders our job is to shut the door, push aside our lunch, and listen. Nothing else matters—not metrics, not selling, not the business.

Yes, we lead teams, and our job is to generate positive results for our company. But remember you're leading humans, and people are dealing with a complex personal life.

Leading is a privilege. Hold space for people when they need it.

Welcome. Why I Wrote This Field Guide:

When you're going about your day, running errands and checking things off your to-do list, you may not notice when a store is running well; you may not notice much about it at all. There were people to help you. You got what you needed, a solution to a question, perhaps. You moved on with your day.

When a store is not running well, you notice right away. It's obvious and can be frustrating.

I'm about to show you how to set up your store so your customers will be happy (although they may not know why) and your bosses will be impressed. Most importantly, your team will feel supported and, in turn, support each other.

You're about to learn all the secrets and best practices of running a retail store. You're about to learn that your team comes first, above all else.

But Wait, Let Me Introduce Myself:

Hey, I'm Kit. I'm a writer and former retail leader. I spent over twenty years leading teams in retail buildings. When I graduated college with a degree in merchandising, I had zero intentions of getting into store leadership. The summer after graduation, I worked as a sales associate for a department store. I thought it would be a good idea to learn the operational aspect of running a store until I worked my way onto glamorous photo shoots. I wanted to be a stylist back then.

Then a funny thing happened. I liked working in store leadership, and I was good at it. Department store work wasn't for me, so I went to work for a boutique in the mall with a small team of associates.

I received keys to a building, and, for the first time, I realized how I could be an integral and positive part of someone's day.

I helped with training and problem-solving. I learned how to think on my feet and be a partner to the sales team. I was hooked. I wanted to keep learning how to do the job better. I wanted to get faster and streamline operational processes. I wanted people to have fun at their jobs.

Tucson, Arizona, is my hometown. I was born and raised there among the saguaros and gila monsters. In 2000, at age twenty-four, I moved to Southern California. I spent over twenty years on a retail sales floor, working my way up through management. In my final retail location, I was a Store Manager; I built teams in that one building for nine years. By the time I left, everyone who worked there was there because of me.

My store was a training ground in the district. Every leader in my building could train a new person to do their job. I was also a resource for the district, often traveling to other stores to support newer teams. I was incredibly proud—this was my goal when I started in this store, and to see it realized was rewarding.

In 2022, I left my retail career to write full time. I knew I could not sustain the physicality of retail forever, and I wanted to be my own boss. A district manager role would've been next for me, but it didn't seem like much of a challenge, just more of the same. It would be much more work, but what would I learn? I'd still be working for someone else and implementing their directives. I wanted more control. I wanted a say. I wanted to be able to travel whenever I wanted.

After two decades of meager raises, long commutes, blood, sweat, laughter, and tears, I was ready to try something new. I knew I could do anything with the skills I acquired in retail leadership. Being a solo entrepreneur was a natural extension of my leadership skill set.

However, leaving my team was one of the most challenging decisions I've ever made. Every day during my last two weeks, I felt like I might throw up. I'm not naturally anxious, but this was next level. I don't regret my decision, but I miss retail every day.

Being a leader on a retail sales floor teaches you extraordinary skills. In this book, I'm sharing all my best practices. You'll learn how to ease into a new team and gain respect immediately, build the culture, and structure your week.

You'll discover that when you put your team first, the rest falls into place. The team is the foundation of the store (not the customers). The team is everything, and your primary job as Store Manager is to support them and get them what they need. When you do, excellent customer service is a byproduct.

I wrote this book for new store leaders; however, many tips apply to every frontline leadership position.

I can't wait for you to get started.

Let's go.

FOUNDATIONS OF LEADERSHIP

C ongratulations, you're a Store Manager. Hooray! You got the job.

If you're feeling a little nervous, that's okay. If you think you may not have all the answers, that's normal—and it's a good thing. You don't have all the answers. Running a store well takes a team, and you'll need partners along the way. Partners who feel empowered to make decisions and lead teams themselves.

I'll let you in on a little secret. Nobody knows what they're doing most of the time. We learn as we go. There's no better way to learn than to get started. When I was a Store Manager, I proudly displayed a nameplate on my desk that read, "I'm pretty sure I have no idea."

None of us do, and that's okay. Leadership will look a little different now because you're in charge. Your leadership style may change slightly. People may become more guarded with you simply because of your title.

You can still be you. Be empathetic and meet people where they are. You're going to do great. Have confidence in your ability to be a partner and a sounding board. Know that it's okay to say, "I don't know." Be sure to follow that with, "I'll find out and let you know," (and do it).

When you're honest with your team, they'll know it. Transparent leaders command respect. If your team understands the reasons behind your direction, they'll keep showing up and staying engaged.

Your job will be challenging, but it should also be fun. Chatting with strangers all day is cool. Learning your business and discovering how you can make an impact daily is unique. You don't get immediate feedback in most jobs; you do on the frontline in retail.

As a leader, it's essential to remain positive and to not take your frustrations out on the team. If you're feeling pressure from your boss or a metric wasn't where you wanted it, communicate that to your team transparently. Example: "Hey, team, I'm feeling the heat about our customer surveys. How can we make them better? What are we missing? I'd love your help."

This states the stressor, invites your team in, and makes them a part of the solution. It gets you out of your head and out of isolation.

If you have a moment of overload, get out of the

building for ten minutes if you can or step off the floor. Running a sales floor can get hectic, and it's okay to take a minute to gather yourself. Take some deep breaths and stay hydrated. This moment will pass, and you will survive. Take care of yourself.

You're not here to make friends. I mean that in the best way possible. You're here to foster culture. I don't want to freak you out, but your team is watching your every move. They do it so they can understand how to do the job and so they can understand how to talk to you when needed.

The team will follow your lead. If you show up on time with a bright outlook and work alongside others on the floor, they will understand the expectation. This doesn't mean you'll never need to vocalize what you want—you will. However, when you model the behaviors you expect, your team is halfway there to understand them.

If you are ten minutes late every day, your team will understand that punctuality isn't important to you. If you're five minutes early, they will.

Remember, your coworkers are not your friends.

It's essential to be friendly. You can make small talk about weekend plans. Still, I'd discourage you from going out for drinks on Saturday night or sharing social media accounts that are super personal. We all bring a particular version of ourselves to work— the version that has an abundance of patience and doesn't swear. You know what I mean. So, it's easier to lead people when they don't know the details about that trip you took to Las Vegas with your best friends. That's all I'm saying.

You can still be yourself with the people you lead, but it's best not to be friends. I certainly want to avoid managing my friends. It can be awkward. It can appear to the rest of the team that you have favorites because you socialize outside of work, and that's not good.

Have a favorite ice cream. Do not have a favorite team member. A clear separation between your professional and personal life is essential as you step into upper management positions. I've never thought, "Oh, I wish I'd revealed more about my personal life to my team." Never. I have felt the opposite, though. I've regretted telling someone too much.

Your job title doesn't make you a leader. Filling out forms doesn't make you a leader. Respect, empathy, and kindness make you a leader. You are a leader if people respect you, regardless of what claims your title makes. Job titles are made up. In fact, they can even be negotiated. I've spent countless hours with Regional Managers, District Managers, and Vice Presidents. Their titles meant nothing. It's how they fought for their teams that mattered. It was their sincerity and their ability to cut the crap.

Never pull rank.

There are more effective ways to lead than pulling rank without explanation. Nobody wants to hear, "I'm the Store Manager, and I said so." People hate that. It's rude and not helpful. If you can't share something because it's confidential, you can say, "This is in the works, and I'll let you know more as soon as I can."

We'll get into team building and culture later, but for now, know this: Your team is composed of humans living their own lives. You don't need to know everything about them, but remember they have lives outside the store, and you must respect their time.

It's essential to see the individuals on your team as whole people.

- Let them go when they're off work.
- Only change their shifts on a published schedule with their permission.
- Texts should not happen unless it's an emergency e.g. "We have to close the store. Please don't come in today."
- Never text someone about a mistake they made (I mean never ever).

When people work under your direction, that doesn't mean you get special access to their time off. If they made a mistake or you need to talk to them, schedule it for the next time they work with you.

Don't take advantage of people.

Employers treat their staff like trash too often. Give people breaks. Give them lunch. Let them rest. Allow mistakes to be made...without judgment, without punishment. No one comes to work thinking they want to do a lousy job. If you stress about small mistakes, your team will stop asking you for help.

Take suggestions from everyone. Yes, everyone. Even if someone is new or young, they can still have a good idea. Maybe you've been in leadership for a few years; that's great! You'll never know everything. It's okay to say no after you've listened. Explain your thought process and thank the person for expressing interest.

Lead from the front.
People don't want to listen to someone who gives them directions from a back room or office. They want their leaders to work alongside them. When you work next to your team, you can see where they struggle and where they soar. You can lend a helping hand, even if it is just getting shoes from the stockroom. They will appreciate that more than you will ever know.

Newsflash—your team is made up of humans. And, you're a human too! How cool is that? We all pretty much want the same things: to feel valued, appreciated, included, and informed. These are basics in the workplace.

How To Take On A New Team

When I worked in retail, I got moved around often. I said yes to everything. Every new assignment, I took. This meant I moved to new buildings and new teams frequently. I didn't realize it at the time, but getting moved around to new locations gave me a killer skill set and confidence.

I've stepped into eleven different teams and had to lead them. I've done this in all positions: Assistant Manager through Store Manager. I did the same thing every time. Nothing about this is complicated; it simply takes patience.

Step into a new team.
Be friendly and observe. Listen. Have the team teach you how they do things. Correct anything that's not good customer service, harmful to others, or illegal. Otherwise, roll with what they're dishing out.

You're there to learn their processes and work alongside them. Do everything with your team, including sweeping, taking out the trash, cashiering, grabbing shoes for customers, all of it. Keep doing these things in the future, but the first two weeks are crucial.

Your team needs to see you working alongside them. If you sweat with them, they will trust you. Get dirty. If you remain in your office during this time, you will appear unapproachable and remain a mystery (you don't want that).

After a week or two, slowly introduce any needed changes. Minor ones. Explain what you're doing. Once the team gets used to that, you can initiate more considerable changes. Explain that too. Put a positive spin on any updates:

- This will save us time.
- This will increase sales.
- This will help us communicate.
- Let's try it. We can always change it if we don't like it.

People will readily accept change if it's explained to them, and they can clearly see the benefit.

The team comes first.
As a leader, your number one job is to take care of the people on your team. Create a safe space for them. This doesn't mean that no one ever gets in trouble or has a coaching conversation; it means you will support them in every way you can. Mistakes are allowed. No question is a dumb question.

People are allowed to be their unique selves as long as they do their jobs, are kind, and are supportive of others.

"I call Kit when I have a question because I know she'll know the answer and won't make me feel dumb." One of my peers said this about me, and it's one of the best compliments I've ever had. When you are open and nonjudgmental, you inspire conversation. When you act like a know-it-all, people will shut down and not call you for help.

Be the person that your peers reach out to when they need help.

Empower Your Team

As a store leader, most of your job should not be kept secret. Transparency is your friend and leads to staff retention. When you approach your role with this mindset, you're two steps ahead of everyone else, and you slowly add time back to your week.

"Nothing I do is secret. If you want to learn how to do something, I'll teach you." I said this often. Creating an environment like this makes you approachable. It makes people feel like they can ask you questions. It shows that you have humility and want to share the store's success with everyone.

It also makes your job easier. You can delegate small tasks to the sales team to take them off your plate entirely. Your goal is to get your team to be largely self-sufficient. For example, we used to pull a sales read every hour. Yes, this is a "manager task"; however, there's no reason a sales associate can't learn how to do that. Teach them where to find the report and how to do the math. That's it. They get to pull the sales read, inform the rest of the team, and now you don't have to do it anymore.

Teach anyone who wants to learn; we don't play favorites here. You just got five minutes of your day back. That's twenty-five minutes a week. Boom! That's a huge win; in retail, every second counts.

Here's another example:

My team had fifty sales associates and five managers. Sometimes the resources we provided for the associates needed to catch up to demand, such as availability forms. High school and college students changed their availability often, and we occasionally needed more forms. (Yes, we still used paper forms, but bear with me.) You can use this example in almost any circumstance. When someone asked me for a form, I would show them where they could find it on the computer and print more. Their task was then to teach two more people how to do it.

This same scenario is used for loading the paper towel dispensers in the bathrooms. Teach someone else how it works. You gain time back by teaching others how to do these small things themselves. You're also letting your team members know you think they are capable and trustworthy, and you're teaching them to take pride and ownership of the store. Everyone is responsible for the success of the business, not only the person at the top. Printing more forms and refilling paper towels take about five minutes each. You just got ten minutes back when you taught your sales team how to do it.

Repeat the above education for any minor task a sixteen-year-old could handle. These small lessons add up to time back in your pocket. It may not seem like much, but it is. Ten minutes a day is fifty minutes a week. Would you rather spend an hour printing forms and filling paper towel dispensers, or would you like to train your team on the floor? You could also revise a schedule, read sales reports, or walk the mall and build connections with fellow retailers.

This type of thinking takes a few more minutes upfront because you have to teach someone how to do it. Many leaders do too much themselves because they perceive it to be faster, but it's not.

When you are short-sighted, you do too much, thinking it will be faster to get it done yourself. When you take a long-sighted view, you understand that spending an extra ten minutes today training someone will give you time back in the future. You'll save countless hours down the line.

Don't rush to DO. Wait, teach, and empower.

Often, Store Managers are working too hard. They pile everything on their plate when they can otherwise mindfully push things off. Your team wants to help you. Your people want to feel connected and show you they're resourceful and self-reliant. Show them how.
"Anyone can answer the phone."
"Anyone can put away supplies."
"Anyone can take out the trash with a manager if you notice it's full."

These are all things I've said numerous times. Teamwork is about all of us. Everyone supports everyone else. We are all allowed to learn, contribute, and get better at our jobs.

Our team is so smart!

When you give people more to do than what their job title tells them they can do, you'll soon start to develop a team that's dedicated, curious, and ambitious. Pretty soon, you'll start hearing, "I got it!" before you have to run over and help. It's an inspiring thing to watch unfold.

My expectations were high, and the team knew it. I was upfront with them. I told them, "Other Store Managers don't have you do this, but I know you're capable."

I let my Lead Sales people call IT, fix register issues, and complete some of the checklists that were technically a "manager" duty. These tasks were not that hard; they only needed to know who to call and where to find the forms.

I allowed my Assistant Managers to handle customer service issues, order supplies, and write schedules. Not all of them, and not right away, but as a leader, you know when people are ready to learn more. A handful of people I worked with knew how to do everything operationally that I did. When I went on vacation, there was a clear direction of ownership, and I could get away without getting a barrage of text messages.

Empowering your team will make your job easier every day of the week.

Customer Service

Customer service is a big part of your job; however, excellent customer service results from a happy and thriving team. Every company has its philosophy and customer service best practices, but there is a baseline for all great customer interactions: human connection and the subtle art of knowing when to leave a customer alone and when to push the engagement.

That's tricky to learn. The best salespeople are masters at body language. They can pick up subtle clues to help them carry the connection forward.

The best leaders can partner the right salespeople with each customer. That takes knowing your staff really well.

I'm a good salesperson, sometimes great, but not consistently great. I hired great salespeople.
I had salespeople who were better at selling than I was. I knew which person could help grandparents and who could help a teenage girl and her mom.

Those situations require a very different skill set. These small nuances will make or break your sales for the month. If you partner the grandparents with someone who doesn't listen, they'll head for the door.

These are invisible skills. The general public doesn't see this happen, but they feel it. When they leave happy, you've done it right. Retail is brimming with this kind of invisible intelligence.

Quick facts:
- Talk to customers like they're your friends.
- Give your opinion. Share your laundry secrets. Connect. People love that stuff.
- Listen closely. People want to be listened to. Let them talk, then act.
- A few open-ended questions can lead to a great shopping experience.
- Be the hero. Make exceptions when needed.
- If you work for a big company and the customer calls and complains, they'll likely get what they want. As you get more familiar with the policies, you'll understand when you can make exceptions to rules on the customer's behalf.
- Partner associates with customers who are a good fit.

Lastly, customers don't get to treat you like dirt. You can ask someone to leave your store if they are abusive or threatening. Partner with your Loss Prevention Manager and ask them what steps they'd like you to take if this situation arises.

Be ready to take action to protect yourself and your

team.

Building Your Community And Culture

As you build your community and culture, it's essential to understand who you are. How your leadership style fits into the overall leadership team is paramount.

What kind of leader are you?

The most common leadership styles are:
1. Democratic Leadership: Taking input from everyone and making a decision.
2. Autocratic Leadership: Making all the decisions without seeking team input.
3. Laissez-Faire Leadership: This is a hands-off approach. Let the team plan out their week and workload.
4. Bureaucratic Leadership: Leading by the book without much wiggle room for flexibility.
5. Servant Leadership: Putting the needs of the team above all else.
6. Transformational Leadership: Expecting the best out of your team and often showing them new ways to grow.
7. Transactional Leadership: This is more of a give-and-take culture. It's often rigid and can stifle innovation.

There are many ways to assess your leadership style. Know that leadership analysis can be beneficial to your leadership team. You may be a combination of leadership styles, and that's okay. Some days you need to flex your style to accommodate different types of work. Most of the time, I was a combination of a servant leader and transformational leader, but on some occasions, I was an autocrat.

Retail often calls for a quick decision, and you have to make it. In my store, we had a version of leadership analysis our company laid out for us. It included four categories of management styles and a quick quiz to help determine which leadership style we each had.

No style is better than the other; they're just different. Analyzing your style and the rest of your leadership team will lead to a deeper understanding and lend to community building. Your leadership team needs to feel confident running the store when you're not in the building.

Analyzing your leadership style is akin to a personality test. It may help you better understand how you lead and also help you identify your blindspots. There are many leadership quizzes you can take online. I enjoyed this one created by Atlassian. It's quick, fun, and you get your results instantly.

https://www.atlassian.com/blog/leadership/find-your-leadership-style-examples

Understand your blind spots.
You're not good at everything. I'm not either. We

need other people to help us with things we're not experts at managing. A blind spot is just something in which you don't naturally excel.

I'm not great at expressing emotion, so I made sure other leaders on my team were good at it. This way, the team was more balanced, and the door to communication was propped open wider.

Party organizing is not one of my strengths. When we had internal promotions, my co-manager led the celebrations. She knew how to source decorations for cheap, and she knew what donuts to buy. That kind of stuff overwhelms me, and I don't enjoy it. She loved it, so I let her do it. She did it better and faster than I could have.

You need all kinds of people on your team.

Think of your culture like *The Muppets.*
Companies spend too much time worrying about culture. Think of your culture like *The Muppets* and include people who are different from you— vastly different. *The Muppets* are a wide array of misfits. Kermit is the operations frog, Fozzie is the emotional support bear, Animal speaks no words but is happy and free, and Gonzo is the stuntman who is also in love with a chicken. Miss Piggy is a demanding diva, yet she harnesses this energy to do good for the group. Somehow this all works.

That's the thing—each character uses their quirks to do good for the group and ensure the others are supported. This is teamwork. This is culture.

Design guru Brian Collins said it best when he was talking about the creator of *The Muppets,* Jim Henson: "Henson realized that his own talent was amplified, accelerated, and colorized by bringing in collaborators that were different. He went out to find people that were infinitely better than he was. What they created was better than what he could've done by himself."

Be the Jim Henson in your store, and you will build a dynamite team. Include upbeat, talented people no matter where they come from. Boom! You're creating your culture.

Attitude is everything. You want optimistic people. When your internet goes down, and you have to fix it yourself while you talk to IT on speakerphone, you will want Positive Polly on the floor to talk to customers. Believe me.

The teams I led were rag-tag groups. They included artists, surfers, nerds, skaters, yogis, and Comic-Con fanatics. You name it. Everyone helped out and did their part because everyone was welcome. Find out what people are good at and use their strengths to the team's advantage.

Not everyone will be a top seller. That's mathematically never going to happen. That's okay because you don't want a store full of top sellers. You want a handful of top sellers that you can schedule at peak times. You also need quiet, organized people. These people can help process shipment and work during floor moves. These people will make your window displays look stunning. Running a successful team means including various personalities and skill sets.

A leader doesn't look a certain way. I promoted young misfits into leadership positions throughout my retail career. Most of these people didn't see themselves as leaders, but they were. They were kind, hardworking, open to learning, and open to helping others. That's a leader!

They thrived because they got to show up daily as their true selves and show me the best parts of themselves. The entire team succeeded. Promoting from within your store boosts morale and engagement in the team.

Get a hype person. Share the love of the store.

Assign one of your leaders to be the hype person of the store. This leader gets excited about contests, new hires, and is motivating. This leader is creative and good at coming up with weekend contests on the fly and decorating the back room. As the Store Manager, I had little time for most of this, so I delegated to someone good at it.

I had a large team and wanted people to feel connected, so I created a photo wall in our hallway. Each team member sent me their favorite photo of themselves. I printed them out in 4"x6" format, backed them with pre-cut cardstock, wrote the person's name and title, and created a collage in the common hallway in the back room.

What does this achieve?

It makes the store feel more cohesive. It makes people feel included. If two people don't know each other, they can glance at the wall, see a photo, and can look out for them later. It feels like a group photo. Everyone is together. It creates a team vibe in the back room. It's uplifting. It's also entertaining to look at the final version and say, "Wow! Look at our awesome team."

The store, including the break room and back rooms, should feel loved. That means clean and bright. Get lights replaced. Fix broken benches or chairs. Make the back room as inviting as possible. Back rooms and break tables can get gross; ensure they don't. Cleaning them should be part of the closing procedures. This is only a five-minute process. Do it daily, and it won't ever get too bad.

Actionable empathy: Fight for your team.
Coming up in my career, I had fantastic Store Managers, and I've had terrible ones. Their titles weren't important. Their candor was. Everything pales in comparison to honesty, kindness, and sincerity. These skills have been called soft skills, emotional intelligence, and people skills. Slightly different phrasing but they mean the same thing. They create the cornerstone of outstanding

leadership. Empathy is included in this. Having empathy doesn't make you weak. It's a killer skill to have.

Empathy means that you understand the people you work with are humans trying to do their best. It means you see them with everything they have on their plate, and you'll do what you can to support them.

Actionable empathy is what makes good leaders great. Actionable empathy is when leaders make the first move and protect their teams' physical and mental health.

Practicing empathy looks like this:

- Listening without interruption
- Paying attention to non-verbal cues
- Asking questions to learn more
- Willing to be vulnerable
- Imagining yourself in someone else's shoes

As I became a tenured Store Manager and knew my team well, I'd proactively protect my team from overworking:

- I'd let team members choose the zones they worked in, so they didn't get fatigued in one area.
- I'd say no when someone wanted to pick up another shift and they were burning out.
- Closing shifts were spread equally between the managers.

When you practice actionable empathy, your team will feel it and understand that you care about them, even if they can't vocalize why. Fear-based leadership is an old-school way of thinking, and it doesn't work. Let your team see that you are human, you make mistakes, but you can say you're sorry, course-correct, and get back up.

Celebrate Success

Look for success everywhere. It's out there and only sometimes tied to a metric.

Success doesn't always mean you made your sales goal for the month. It could mean a Senior Associate did a great job training a new person. It can also mean that someone took initiative, completed a task quickly, or had an outstanding customer interaction.

Sometimes success is simply getting through the day without a call-out or injury. Sometimes it's working as a team even when everyone is tired and wants to go home and take a nap.

See success in everything.
Say please and thank you often, and do it genuinely. "Please" and "thank you" must be extensions of your everyday language. Be specific.

"Natascha, thank you for taking over my customer so
I could help the customer on hold."

"Alex, thanks for boxing those hangers so quickly and
cleaning the cash wrap. I appreciate it."

"Sammy, can you do me a favor and pull these shirts off the floor, please? We have to send them out. Thanks!"

People will feel good and continue to do it. It makes them feel seen.

Is this their job? Yes. Are you juggling more than them? Probably. It doesn't matter, though. It's not about you. When you lead people, the goal is to lift them and show them how the work they do everyday matters.

When you do this regularly and then need to have a coaching conversation, your team is more receptive because most of your feedback has been good. They understand you have their best interest at heart. When you say, "Hey, Alex, we've talked about you running late. Please be on time for your next shift, or we'll have to move to documentation," it won't sting so much.

Success is understanding reality. Success is variable. There may come a time when you're short-staffed, burnt out, and have a call out. You're exhausted, and your team is too. However, it's Saturday, and you must be ready for business.

Success means rallying the team and saying,"Today, we're going to do our best and have fun. We'll help each other out and not take ourselves so seriously. We're going to get to the other side today, and we're going to go to bed early. Let's do this."

Some days we have big wins, and other days getting to the end of our shift is a success. No two days are the same. Success looks different every day. Today's success doesn't look like yesterday's success. Keep moving.

Find time to laugh with everyone.

I don't need to tell you, but running a retail store can be insane. People call out, or you get a rush out of nowhere. What just happened? Connect with your team and share a laugh when you get a breather. It will bring you together and break the tension.

A few years ago, we were preparing for a regional visit during one very hectic day at work. One of the guys who worked in shipment, Edgar, found a mismatched shoe. This was a big deal. We got in trouble for having mismatches, and no one had time to research it and find the other shoe that day. My co-manager and I were running through the store, preparing for the visit.

"What should I do with this shoe?" Edgar asked us.

"Hide that thing, fool!" My co-manager yelled as she zoomed by. I stopped and laughed so hard I was crying.

Be a human.

What it comes down to is being a human. You can laugh at work and have fun even when things feel crazy. And yes, we found the missing shoe after the visit.

Organizing Your Office, Backroom, And Break Room

Let's set up your back room.

Your sales floor will only run correctly if your back rooms are clean. They are interconnected. If you have product in stock rooms, it needs to be organized daily as you receive new shipment. The team needs to understand how it's organized. If organization slips, you'll miss sales.

The Merchandiser/Visual Manager can keep hardware neat and inform the team about the organization. This department gets wild quickly. Tidy it up daily. It's everybody's responsibility to put things away correctly and keep the store organized. This isn't your house. Anyone on your team should be able to walk in the back and find what they need. The same goes for the management office.

Any shared space should be hyper-organized. Fifty employees could move stuff all over the store throughout the week. Everything needs to have a place. My store was much more organized than my house. Create a personal space for each leader if you have a shared management office. This step seems small, but it's essential. We had cubbies for our stuff and file folders for any needed paperwork. People feel they belong when they have a place for their stuff (the floor is an unacceptable long-term option).

Bulletin boards and whiteboards are your friends. Keep lists in plain view. Anything you're actively working on should be posted for the team to see. It will keep you all on track. Active lists do you no good when they're in a binder. They need to be visible daily. If something important is not written down somewhere you can see it every day, you'll probably forget about it. Out of sight, out of mind is real, friends. I used this plain-view tactic for our hiring goals.

Hiring goals: We had to hire about twenty seasonal sales associates every peak season. That is about four to five people a week leading up to the peak. It takes careful coordination.

I'd write out our hiring goals on a whiteboard in the office like this:

Goal: 20
Week one: 4 people
1.
2.
3.
4.
Week two: 5 people
Etc.

My hiring manager would fill in the names as she hired people. It worked well, and I could see, at a glance, if we were on track.

Use this for supply lists too. Use a whiteboard or a bulletin board. Create a new list every week. Once a week, place your order and create a new list. This way, anyone can add to the list. If your opening associate notices the store is getting low on glass cleaner, they can add it to the list.

Bulletin boards

If you have the space and enough bulletin boards, assign them like the following:

1. Scheduling
   - This week's and next week's schedules
     - Post anything schedule-related, like time-off requests or availability changes. If your employees can access this online, post the directions here. Ensure your team knows that time off requests and availability changes need approval. A submission doesn't equal approval. Post your approval schedule as well so they know what to expect. Example: "I approve all requests on Mondays. If your request is denied, I will reach out to you. Otherwise, consider it approved."
   - Blackout calendar
     - Any blocks of time that cannot accommodate multiple days off, such as holiday time, should be posted here. You can print a blank calendar, highlight the blackout days, and post a note such as "Hey, team, the company has determined these days as a blackout. Please be aware we cannot approve time off for more than two days in a row." Now your team understands why, and they know they can still request

a day off if needed. (Two-week trips to Hawaii will not be approved over the Christmas holiday.)

2. Management scheduling

- Same as above, but it's in the manager's office.

3. Operations

- I kept this bulletin board next to our manager's computer. It had the company calendar posted with all the events for the next few weeks, the payroll breakdown for the current week, and the supply list. As managers processed payroll each morning and edited time cards, they could quickly see what was going on and if we were on track with our payroll. They could also see what hours we were allocated for each department. The supply list was posted here for ease of use.

4. The Fun One

- We kept a bulletin board next to our break table for encouraging notes. Any team member could write a public message to someone else. Examples include thanking them for their help, congratulating them on a big sale, etc. It's crazy fun when your team starts to support each other.

- Motivation does not always come from leaders; it also comes from peers. We kept cardstock, markers, and stickers handy.

The team could get creative. By the end of the month, it would be full of colorful and inspiring notes.

- At the end of the month, associates could take the notes home.

Team recognition

Retail leadership can feel insane. I know you know. You go in for the day with your agenda, and after you've put your stuff away and run your payroll numbers, your day gets flipped upside down. Memos and emails come flooding in and you get a call from your District Manager.

Welp, there goes your plans for the day.

You say yes to all that is asked of you because that's what we do here. We say yes to everything. Sometimes we're so busy we forget to slow down and appreciate all the people who work in our buildings. Employee of the Month posters are posted yet scantily filled out. Break tables get dirty. We're too busy rushing to fit in one more thing for the day that we forget about the person working right next to us.

I get it. I've been there. Slow down for ten minutes and ensure your team is well taken care of, then you can get back to running a mile a minute.

Spell and pronounce your employees' names correctly.

I know what you're thinking. Duh, Kit. However, this is a common mistake.

For a couple years, I had two associates who looked very similar. They were both hired around the same time. I got their names wrong for about two weeks. I called Tierra by Lannie's name and Lannie by Tierra's name more often than I'd like to admit. They thought it was funny because I was trying yet kept getting it wrong.

If I hadn't tried, and blown off the mistake, hilarity would've turned into resentment. It would've meant that I didn't care enough about them as humans to get their names correct.

We're often so busy rushing through our day that we grab a notecard or write something down on our zone chart, and we spell someone's name wrong, or we may say it incorrectly. Not a huge deal, but employees feel valued when we get it right. It's not a huge deal unless you get it wrong every time. It's a huge deal if you don't try to get it right. Especially when someone has a unique name, spell it and say it correctly. Apologize when you get it wrong, and let them know you'll practice it.

I minored in public relations in college, and I'm going to be honest with you, I don't remember much of what I learned, but what I do remember is to ensure that you spell people's names correctly. It was like the ultimate faux pas if you got it wrong.

Don't get it wrong repeatedly.

Create a place in the back room for team recognition. The fun bulletin board is an example, but I'd recommend doing more than that. Next to our employee lockers, we created a space to highlight our employee of the month. The person got a framed certificate hung up and a special lanyard to clip their name tag on. However you decide to celebrate people, make it fun and memorable. (There's nothing sadder than walking into a back room and their employee of the month poster is empty.)

Create a spot to celebrate top sales performers. Each week, we would highlight the top salesperson in key metrics such as:
- Top Sales
- Top Average Dollar Sale (ADS)
- Top Units Per Transaction (UPT)
- Most Positive Customer Surveys

It can be whatever you want, but ensure you keep it current. You could also highlight the top shipment person or the fastest cashier.

Never call anyone out publicly who may need improvement. Do not post a note that reads, "Why are you always at the bottom, Steven? Do better." Nope. Team recognition is for upbeat celebrations only. Show your appreciation consistently.

Ditch the threatening notes.
When I visited stores, I saw some crazy

communication. I walked into a shoe stockroom once, and there was a note on the door that read, "You MUST put away shoes correctly. If you don't, you'll be WRITTEN UP." Let's take a step back. Would you want to work in an environment like this? Probably not. I understand why this note went up. I feel the frustration behind the words; however, this is not the answer.

What to do?
Does everyone know how the stock room is organized? Let's start there.

- Create a list of names of everyone on your staff.
- Speak to each person about the organization. Have them explain to you how the shoe room should be organized.
- Once you know they understand, they sign by their name.

Will this forever keep the stock rooms organized? No, but you've now made it a focus and checked for understanding. Once a week, if your traffic is slow, send an associate back to tidy up any shoe boxes gone rogue.

The solution is a team effort. Threatening notes can lead to the opposite outcome you desire.

YOUR TYPICAL WEEK

When I first stepped into one of my stores as a Store Manager, I was writing the management schedule. I started a conversation with the co-manager and told her she'd have the weekend off. She looked like she was going to cry. "I've never had a Sunday off," she said. "I think I'm going to like working with you." I was astonished. "Well, you'll get at least one off a month now," I replied.

Being fair is an underrated leadership quality. Being fair boosts morale and engagement. It lets your team know that you care about their well-being. Creating a "typical week" scheduling system will support fairness among the group. Creating a typical week for yourself will set you up for success as a Store Manager, even if you can't stick to it every week. It will give you a baseline to work from, and you can flex when necessary. It will provide you with a place to start.

Here is a schedule I followed as a Store Manager that worked well for me:
- Sunday: off
- Monday: open

- Tuesday: close
- Wednesday: open
- Thursday: off
- Friday: close
- Saturday: open

I also ensured I worked one Sunday a month, which will throw off your typical week a little, but it's okay.

Did this typical week work every week? No. I still had to shift my schedule to work on special projects; however, following a schedule like this is a good baseline. Here's why:

- Sunday: This is usually a shorter day. No communication from corporate is coming down, so it's a good day for the SM to be off.
- Monday: ALL the communication from corporate hits the stores. The sales floor is usually slow, so it's a good time to use this day for planning. Monday is an ideal office day. (If any corporate leaders are reading this, your Store Managers need an office day. They need one day a week off the floor. Help them make it a reality.)
- Tuesday: You get to work with different sales associates, and you can understand your weeknight traffic.
- Wednesday: Run the sales floor. Work with your other leaders and associates.
- Thursday: A break after three days is incredible. You're going to want it. Then,

when you go back to work, you only have two days, then you're off again.

- Friday: You're headed into the weekend. Be there for the increase in traffic and to set yourself up for Saturday.
- Saturday: You know what you're walking into because you closed Friday night. This is usually the last day of the week to earn your payroll or to make your weekly sales goal —rally—go, go, go. Sell, work alongside the team, and have fun.

When I wrote my management schedule, I'd write my shifts first using this typical week format. I'd adjust my shifts based on the needs of the business, vacation accommodation, etc. Writing your schedule this way ensures that you're there for the most critical days of business and that you get to work with everyone on your team. It also ensures equality.

Be fair. Don't subject one leader to work every Sunday while you take every Sunday off. It's not cool. Sticking to a typical week will ensure the workload is spread evenly throughout the leadership team. It will also lend itself to a more flexible management team. Bend, don't break.

Writing a good schedule can streamline your week and make your store more money.

Anyone can plug in shifts using availability forms, but that's different from what makes a good schedule. First, use all your allocated hours. Schedule all of them. Do not leave any on the table. Cut later in the week if you have to, but do not under-schedule—it makes everyone's life harder.

Next, pay attention to who you schedule and when. It's where you zone your associates that matters. Yes, anyone can open the store. Gathering trash and cleaning doesn't require much training, but you don't want anyone. You want a person who is thorough, self-motivated, and upbeat in the morning.

No leader wants to open the store with a night owl. They're not so great early in the day. Some people aren't morning people, and that's okay. Schedule them later in the day. They are your closers.

Work alongside your team and get to know them.
That sounds obvious, right? Well, many leaders don't do it. Then they wonder why the store is dirty every day. It's because you keep scheduling Alex to open, and Alex isn't at his best early in the morning.

Talk to people. Work next to them. Ask them what they like about the job or what they'd like to learn. Stop scheduling the associates who call out to open. Schedule them as a mid-shift. That way, if they call out, it won't ruin your day. Take what your team tells you and write the best schedule ever. This is their store, too. A well-planned schedule is the secret to boosting your business.

Outstanding leadership is the culmination of a lot of tiny interactions.
These small interactions are like grains of sand that, when gathered together, make up the beach that supports your blanket. The subtle art of knowing your team well enough to write an amazing schedule that works for them and for you is what makes good leaders excellent.

Priority Order

Priority order can take plenty of work to grasp at first. This can be a tough one. Becoming a Store Manager can feel like the weight of the entire building is sitting on your shoulders. It doesn't have to be like that.

Each day, do what only you can do first—scheduling, fixing payroll issues, interviewing, etc. After your job is squared away, you can help in shipment, on the floor, or with whatever else needs to get done. Remember that you will only finish some of what you need to do in a day, and that's okay. You'll have some things roll into the next day. Focus on what you have to get done now, and roll the rest.

I never left my store at the end of my shift and thought, "Wow, I got everything finished today. Hooray!" No. I usually left thinking, "I got the important stuff done. Tomorrow, I'll take care of the rest."

Pay people correctly.

Ensure your payroll is 100% accurate. The opening manager can edit time cards daily, but the Store Manager needs to check them before they are submitted.

People work because they need money, not because they love you. A sure way to show your team that you respect them is to ensure they're being paid accurately.

Best practice: Grab your zone chart (or schedule) from the previous day. As you edit time cards, put a checkmark next to the employee's name on the zone chart. This way, you can see everyone. If someone worked but forgot to clock in and out, you may not notice. You'll immediately catch that mistake if you see their name on the zone chart. Was sick time entered correctly? If it wasn't, fix it. Fix it right now. That's your priority. Did a sales associate help another location and the company pays for mileage? Make sure they get it. This is priority number one.

Paying people accurately is the baseline for earning respect from your team. It's the first line in advocating for people. It's important.

Did I mention that it's important? Okay, cool. Now, let's stay on track.

How To Stay On Track.

Keep a to-do list daily to keep you on track. Keep it in your pocket, or use your phone. Whatever works. I liked to use a piece of scrap paper. When I write stuff in my own handwriting, I remember it better. I also really enjoy crossing things out with a pen.

I would put a star next to it or the letter "A" for anything that had to happen today. Any task that would be nice to get done today got the letter "B," and so on.

As the Store Manager, we must ensure our job gets done. Our Job. I know that sounds obvious and oversimplified, but check it out:

- Have you hired enough people? Are you fully staffed?
- Have you communicated thoroughly with your other leaders?
- Is your staff schedule complete?
- Are people getting paid correctly and on time?

Yes, everything in my store is my job, but only I can do specific things. I need to make sure those get done. Whatever stuff your support managers don't have access to—get that stuff done.

You'll get it.
After you practice this for a few weeks, it will become a habit. You won't have to think so much about priority order because you'll be used to doing the important tasks first, and you won't get lost in all the things. You'll have to shift your priority order

all the time. Like, all...the...time. That's okay. That's a part of your job. When your District Manager calls last minute with something you need to do immediately, you'll know what task you can bump to the next day because you'll have your list.

Switch it around. Lists are made to be changed. They're flexible. To-do lists are in constant motion, just like you. If you get overwhelmed, go back to the basics.

Pay people correctly, ensure your job is complete before you do anything else, then help with the rest.

For your sanity -
Keep a running list of items and processes that are and are not working. Notebook, email, app, whatever. That way, when your District Manager calls, you won't forget. Otherwise, you'll forget, believe me. She'll call you randomly, and you'll say, "Oh yeah, everything is great!" You'll listen to her and then hang up the phone, immediately remembering the laundry list you need to talk to her about. I can't count the number of times I hung up the phone after talking to my DM and was like, "Dammit."

Communication: Keep Everyone Informed

Clear, concise communication is the bedrock of an efficient team.

No matter what size team you lead, communication must be front and center every day. Yep, it's not sexy, but this is how you get through the weeks without drowning. I know this sounds super basic, but many teams I went to help didn't do this. Their support leaders were opening the store and running the floor, but they had no concept of the business at large. They lacked the understanding of how things fit together.

Transparency will cure many things. A daily communication log will help your leadership team see the business globally. They'll begin to understand all that needs to happen and how they fit into it.

Often, your staff doesn't understand why you're stressed out. They see you walking back and forth to the office and taking phone calls. They see you at a computer. They don't really know what you're doing all day. If you haven't lived it, it doesn't translate. You look busy, but that's all they know. So, tell them.

"I have to cut this conversation short; I have to get on a conference call with the other managers in the district to discuss back-to-school planning."

Tell your team what you're up to. They want to know. They want to help with what they can. The more you're able to feed them these bits of information, they will start to put together a picture of what your job entails. It's good for everyone.

Written communication is essential to keeping the day on track and keeping all leaders informed on the day-to-day nuances of running a store. Written communication among your leadership team needs to happen every day, all day, not only at closing.

In my store, we had one email for the store that all leaders shared; we didn't have our own company email addresses. If you have another place where leaders can leave notes—in a store app, maybe—great! Make sure it happens. Set the expectation that leaders leave notes throughout the day. As soon as the day begins, the communication begins.

Our daily written communication looked like this: The opening manager begins a new email with today's date and hits save. Managers update this email all day long with the facts as they unfold.
- AC broke—tech will be out tomorrow.
- Jenny called out. Rachel is covering for her.
- Tommy cleaned the bathrooms and stocked the cash wrap for tomorrow.
- Some kid stole a skateboard. I submitted an LP report.

Stick to the facts. You can follow up in person if you have feelings about a situation. The daily email is only about communicating what happened, what was completed, and what still needs to get done. It's not for assigning blame, being snarky, or making yourself into the hero.

Refrain from reprimanding a leader through shared

written communication.
"Stacy, why didn't you gather the trash last night?!!!!
Come talk to me."

Aw, hell no. Not cool. Instead, leave a note like this:
"Stacy, I have a question for you. Please remind me
to ask you when you arrive today." Address Stacy in
person and ask her what happened with the trash.

When you do it in written communication, you're
yelling at this person in front of their peers. That is
awkward and disrespectful. Your team will begin to
lose respect for you if you continue.

Similarly, do not text people when they are off the
clock unless it's an emergency. If you have the urge
to text someone, tell them they did a great job
today. If your text is not congratulatory, don't do it
—respect people's time off. Leading people does not
give you special access to people. Do not expect
people to receive or respond to your messages
outside of the building. Reprimanding someone
over a text message is rude and cowardly. It's also
one of the fastest ways to make people lose respect
for you.

Should you text someone when they're off?
Ask yourself, is this 411 or 911?

411 vs. 911— Respect time away from work
Before we all carried cell phones with us at all times,
we had the pleasure of calling 411.

411 was a direct information line. You could call 411

to get an address or a phone number. It was faster than lugging out the phone book and was a general shortcut to information.

Why am I telling you this? Because if you're about to reach out to a team member when they're off the clock, you need to ask yourself, "Is this 411 or 911?" You can wait if it's a 411 situation and you only need information. You can ask someone else or call another store.
If it's 911, a true emergency, then you can text them or call them.

Teach your team this too. When you've trained your leaders to be self-sufficient, they shouldn't need to text you when you're off work. Let them know where their resources are and whom to call when you're off.

Too often, Store Managers get texts all day long that are 411-related.
- Do we have more printer paper?
- Was the schedule submitted?
- Can I request Tuesday off?

When your leadership team uses written communication daily and your store is hyper-organized, the need for this 411 communication should dwindle.

Store Managers should always be open to 911 calls. This may include:
- We have a surprise visit tomorrow.
- The mall is closing the North entrance in the

morning.

- Can you open tomorrow instead of close? Max is sick.

When your District Manager calls the store, any leader who answers the phone should be able to answer her basic questions about the business or about what's happening in your shopping center.

Daily communication will ensure you're all on the same page. Note that if your leadership team is this capable, it will make you look super awesome. Store Managers who lead self-sufficient teams with transparency are gold. Your District Manager knows it.

Delegate: Divisions Of Responsibility

Divisions of responsibility (DORs) will keep your leadership team on track and give them something to own. Many retail companies use the term DOR. It's straightforward and easy to understand, so I'm using it here.

DORs will lead to empowerment.

Your leadership team needs to know what they're in charge of. Be clear about it. Have conversations with them individually and let them know what they will oversee. When you have a new leader or someone new in a DOR, a weekly checklist can be helpful to keep them on track.

Leaders could work in their DOR for a year. That was my goal. You want your leaders to be an expert in the department before you move them on to the next one. However, if your team is moving like lightning, you could move them after six months.

Talk to them and listen to their feelings about their proficiency and what they want to learn. Leaders typically learn the Operations DOR quickly and need more time in the Hiring/Training DOR.

The following breakdown works well if you have four managers:
- Operations
- Hiring & Training
- Visual & Merchandising
- Store Manager (The Store Manager oversees everything and lends a hand to each department when needed.)

If you have more than four leaders, assign two leaders to each DOR. You'd likely have a department lead and a supervisor. If you have fewer leaders, the Store Manager will own one of the DORs. You could also combine Operations & Hiring/Training if you have a smaller team.

Get your leaders what they need to do their jobs, and get out of their way.

Let people do their jobs. Let them mess up.
Now that your team knows what's going on, let them do their jobs. Give them permission to make

a mistake. Sure, they could always text you, but that should be for emergencies only. When the leadership team understands where their resources are, they won't text you on your day off.

When you come back into the business, celebrate all the success. If something could've been done more efficiently, let your team know but do it in a relatable way. "Oh, yep. I totally get why you did that. That's okay. Next time, you can do XYZ and save some time."

The pace and relentless pressure of being a retail leader can get overwhelming. If someone messes up, the last thing they need is to be afraid of you. People will also quit taking initiative and stop taking the reins if they're afraid they will get yelled at for messing up. Let them work. It will make your life easier even if you have to do some coaching along the way.

Whenever I had new leaders, they would goof up the change order when they were first doing it. The Guarda employee would show up at our store to deliver the change with $50 in pennies, shaking his head because he knew it was a mistake. We'd have a laugh and joke about how we wouldn't need pennies for a while. Once the new leader saw what $50 in pennies looked like, they never made that mistake again. "It's no biggie." I'd tell them. "Now, you know."

People are more capable than you think. They

learn quickly. When I led teams, I treated my Lead Sales Associates like Assistant Managers and my Sales Associates like Lead Sales. Once they were comfortable in their position and with the company policies, I empowered them to take more ownership over the store. I trained them like this so they could handle anything that came their way. It prepared them for pop-in visits from corporate and for unhappy customers and made them resourceful.

Most companies have a breakdown of what each DOR includes, but here is a general guide.

DOR CHART

DIVISIONS OF RESPONSIBILITY

OPERATIONS
- Change orders
- Checklists
- Online/In store orders (omni-channel)
- Filing
- Back room posters
- Supply orders
- Work orders & IT issues
- Loss Prevention training
- Employee recognition

VISUALS
- Store standards
- Read visual updates
- Window displays
- Work during floor moves
- Remerchandising from sell-thru
- Keep hardware neat & organized
- Receive shipment
- Back of house
- Employee recognition

HIRING & TRAINING
- Post jobs
- Interview
- Candidate communication
- New hire orientations
- Guest experience training
- Employee files
- Ongoing training
- Lockers
- Name tags
- Employee recognition

STORE MANAGER
- Oversee all DORs
- Write schedules
- Manage time off & availability requests
- Networking & recruiting
- Succession planning
- Touch base with dept. leaders daily/weekly
- Own a dept. if there isn't a leader to cover it
- Employee recognition

Operations

Operations is a great starting point if you have a newer leader. Overseeing this department gives them an overall view of how the store runs. They'll learn where all their resources are and whom they can call when something breaks or doesn't work (because that will happen the first time they close alone).

A tenured Operations Manager could add schedule writing to their plate.

Visuals

This department includes store standards, recovery, and building walls using the fixtures unique to your store. Leaders will learn how to read a visual update, how to flex merchandise depending on store inventory levels, and how to fill holes when an item sells through. In this department, window displays and backstock organization are essential skills to learn.

Hiring & Training

Hiring & Training is the most challenging department to run, so this should go to experienced leaders. Endless rules and regulations have to be followed. Each state has its own set of rules and so does the federal government. If you're hiring minors (those under eighteen) in California, you're in for a slew of additional rules.

It's really easy to get something wrong and not be in legal compliance. Hence, a senior leader should run this in close partnership with the Store Manager. The hiring manager schedules and conducts interviews, facilitates orientation and onboarding, maintains employee files, and ensures ongoing training.

Share ownership in the store.
Once the leaders are off and running and sure of their DORs, you can begin to have some of your more seasoned associates share the workload. Have tenured sales associates "own" part of the store. Break down quick, manageable tasks that salespeople can work on between customers.

We had cases with sunglasses and watches. They were usually dirty—fingerprints on the glass and dusty shelves. It felt impossible to make time to clean this area. I'd assign the cases to a sales associate who wanted to do more.

Once a week, during downtime, clean the cases. I'd tell them to ask me if they could do it rather than waiting for my direction because, honestly, I'd probably forget. People were happy to oblige and to make a small, special contribution to the store on their shift. They'd gain product knowledge, and the small task would keep them busy during a lull in traffic.

Because of this small delegation, I didn't have to worry about the cases anymore. When my District Manager walked in unannounced, I looked like a superstar.

After you've led your team for a while, and you have some sales associates who are thriving and want to move up, you can add these people to help with some aspects of the DOR. Every leader could use help printing, copying, and organizing.

How To Multitask

Generally, customer needs come before any other task. Yes, your employees are the most important people in your building, but your customers are a close second.

I had a loyal customer base because people knew we'd go out of our way to help them. We'd call another store, order online, and get them on their way quickly. Only make people wait if you have to. Don't have a team meeting on the sales floor while you have a line of customers at the cash wrap. Your customers don't understand what you're doing and why you're not helping them.

It's not always what you're doing, it's what it looks like you're doing. To the untrained eye (customers), a team huddling on a busy day looks like you're not working and you all are just goofing around.

During peak season, if I had enough floor coverage, I would give associates their five-minute chat-in (at the start of their shift) in the back room. In this way, I could be thorough, they could ask questions, and we could get out on the floor quickly. We didn't have to worry about customers interrupting us. If you have enough people during peak seasons, try it.

Keep flexing

In retail, we flex all day long. We're good at it.

If you've worked retail for a few years, you're probably good at multitasking. Whenever I shop at Ulta, I see one cashier using two registers to ring up two customers in close succession. She doesn't miss a beat. It's impressive. Retail people always do stuff like this without even thinking about it. It's in our blood. Now that you can multitask like the best, ensure that you teach your team the tips that got you so good at it.

What to say

Breakaway statements: When you're helping multiple customers, and your store is busy, breakaway statements are a lifesaver. These statements let your customer know that you know what you're doing and that you'll be back.

"I'll let you browse the shoe wall, and I'll be back to check on you."
"The women's denim is over here. I'm going to get a size for someone, and I'll be right back."

Tell the customer:
- What to look at
- Where you're going
- When you'll be back

When you do this, customers will be stoked every time. You look like a hero.

Delegate and always communicate. When it's too busy, and you're swamped, ask for help and delegate. Make sure you tell your customer what's happening.

"I'll be right back after I get this size."
"James is on his way to help you."
"I'm going to call Nicole over. She's the expert here."

Customers are humans too.
People are usually more than willing to wait if you've filled them in on what's happening. If you get overwhelmed, shut down, and don't talk to your customers, they'll be confused and feel forgotten. Then they may get impatient or angry.

Customers can see how busy you are. They'll feel cared for and seen when you let them in on your plan. Keep them in the loop, and they'll be happy.

Vendor Partnerships

"Vendor partnerships" is a fancy way of talking about the people you do business with who don't work for your company.

You encounter people all day long who support your business, and you want to maintain a good relationship with them.

Whom am I talking about?
- Delivery drivers: UPS, FedEx, USPS, etc.
- Mall management
- Other leaders and employees from other stores in your center
- Representatives from brands you may carry

It's in your best interest to be kind and understanding to all these people. This may seem obvious, but I used to hear our delivery drivers gripe about which stores were not friendly to them. By the way, delivery drivers know all the gossip and aren't worried about who they tell.

Remember, you're not better than anyone else because you have keys to a building or the title of Store Manager. Honestly, most people won't care what your title is. What they will care about is how kind you are. Everyone on this planet is trying to earn a living so they can live their best life. Make people's day easier if you can.

Be kind and patient. Get to know people's names. Please don't yell at them when they make an unexpected delivery or dump an extra shipment at your door. That's not their fault. They're just doing their job, and they have zero control over what you get sent.

If you're rude or grumpy with people, they'll remember. If you're cool to them and talk to them like humans, they'll remember that too.

Drivers, mall managers, and other mall employees liked coming to our store because we were friendly to all of them. We cared about them. Then, when we needed to borrow bolt cutters from Ulta (true story), they were down to help us. When we asked the FedEx driver to deliver to a different door, he didn't mind.

Creating supportive vendor partnerships is a part of building the community in which you operate. When you do this successfully, the support will flow both ways.

Correspondence

Email and phone etiquette seem apparent; however, when you see or hear someone doing it well, you realize how important it is.

Here's a quick rundown of how to do it well.

Email
Email correspondence should be quick and direct yet thorough.

"Hey, Cindy,

The window set is complete, and we're ready for the

sale tomorrow."

Thanks,
Kit C. @ Store #1234

Follow that format for almost everything you write, and you'll be on the right track. Your boss and corporate partners want the facts, and they want them fast.

Phone
Most companies have a way they'd like you to answer the phone. Follow whatever they tell you. It's probably something along the lines of:

"Thank you for calling Banjo Barn; this is Jenna. How may I help you?"
Or, "Banjo Barn, this is Jenna."

Both are widely accepted. Stating your name is helpful not only to your customers but to your bosses as well. When someone only says the store where they work, "Banjo Barn," it can come across as curt or rude.

If you are busy and cannot help the customer on the phone right away, ask them to be placed on hold.

"May I put you on hold, please?"
The customer will usually say yes.

If you're ringing another customer, try not to answer the phone. If you have to, do this:
- Excuse yourself from the customer you're

ringing up: "Excuse me, one moment, let me just grab the phone."

- Give the customer on the phone a chance to speak. If they have a question that you can answer quickly, do it.
- If it's going to require more attention, ask the customer if you can put them on hold while you finish ringing or find another person to help them.

If you have adequate staff on the floor, assign one person to grab the phone when it rings. That way, you're all clear on who will get it, and you're not all trying to answer it at once.

ASSESSING AND BUILDING TALENT

T eams that thrive and see continued success involve every person. There typically isn't a star. Someone is behind the wheel, but good leaders involve everyone.

Understanding the associates on your team and learning what they're good at takes cooperation from the entire leadership team. Listen to the voices in the room here. Involve all leaders. People work differently for you than they do the other leaders in the building. That's normal. That's okay. Listen closely.

How to assess the sales team -
During a store leadership meeting, about once a month, have a short conversation about the sales team. I used to grab a printed schedule and go down the list, reading one name at a time.

Take one minute to discuss each person. This gives you a chance to talk about your sales team openly and honestly so that you can identify their characteristics and attributes. You can assess their skill set as a team.

Like this:

Jaime—Great cashier. Patient. Slow at go-backs. Usually five minutes late.

Amy—Positive attitude, quick pace, fantastic style, a frontrunner for a Lead Sales position.

Joey—Great in the shoe department, gets distracted by other sales associates easily, still learning how to cashier.

Notice that this feedback is constructive and doesn't include the word "favorite" or "I don't like her." Why? The word "favorite" is toxic and does a tremendous amount of damage. It doesn't matter if you like a person or not; you need to work with them and forge a partnership, not hang out.

Listen closely to your other leaders as you go through the list. When your Assistant Manager tells you that Betty ignores her direction, believe her. Don't brush it off because Betty works well when you're around.

Unsure about assessing someone? Ask these questions: Is this team member making your job easier or harder? How are they making your job easier or harder? That will take you to the answer quickly. Once you've answered these questions, you'll see their characteristics and attributes clearly. From here, you can use this information to write better schedules.

Maybe you work with Jaime and show her how to get go-backs done more quickly, you can partner Joey with another associate who can finish his cashier training with him, and the next time you work with Amy, you can begin to show her how to run the sales floor.

These management meetings and team assessments are the key to sharpening your team's skills and steering your team bus in the right direction. If you have an associate struggling or seems miserable, let them know it's okay if they leave. You can do this in an empathetic way. Have coaching conversations with them first, but it's okay if the job isn't a fit for them.

Sometimes my teen associates would need help with all they had on their plate. They would occasionally get their schedule wrong, show up late, or be distracted. I'd always say, "I understand you have a lot of things that demand your attention. This job doesn't have to be your number one priority but needs to be on the list."

Encourage people to move on.
Leaders who push people to be loyal to them and get upset when associates want to request time off or quit usually don't build self-sufficient teams that thrive. You want to encourage your team members to keep moving, including out of your store. This seems counterintuitive, but hear me out.

People won't work at your store forever. In fact, they probably shouldn't. Team members will move up and probably out of your building to work at a different location, work with new teams, and continue to grow. That's all good. Some may move into a new field. This is also good. You want to avoid tying people down to this one job. If they're interested in pursuing other things, help them do it.

Think of leadership as a springboard. People will gather under your leadership. You'll have highs and lows. You'll learn and grow together, and then one day, the team member will soar to new heights and dive into another pool.

Encourage this; champion other people's passions.

Let people quit.
Let people resign from your building in an open and supportive way. Having people quit is normal as long as you're not churning through entire store teams every six months.

It's common for people to get quite anxious when they're thinking about leaving a job. They don't want to disappoint you. They may think you'll be mad at them when, in fact, quitting is often good for you and for them.

It's good for them because they can now pursue whatever they dream of doing. It's good for you because now you have a spot on your team for someone new—someone who really wants to be there and is totally psyched about the opportunity.

When fantastic associates leave, it's bittersweet. I'd always encourage these people to come back if they wanted to for seasonal work. They'd be sad to leave the team and nervous about the new adventure, but that's part of life.

Embrace the uncertainty, and you'll wind up somewhere great. Inspire this in your team.

How to release seasonal hires -
If you're hiring a group of people to help you through a peak season like summer or winter, be clear about when their position ends. I would tell people when they were hired when the end of the season was. We typically kept a few seasonal hires on as part-time employees after the season, so we were transparent about who was offered a part-time spot and who would be leaving at the end of the season.

We had two versions of a thank you letter. One thanked the seasonal employee for their hard work and let them know when their last day would be as well as their last paycheck. The other letter offered the seasonal employee a part-time position.

I signed every letter. Each one had an extra handwritten note thanking the employee for their hard work and dedication. These letters were all delivered on the same day. They were sealed in envelopes and taped to the employees 'lockers. The leaders in the building wouldn't tell anyone who was offered a part-time spot or who wasn't. The sales associates would find out first, and then they could share the news.

Crush gossip where you can. Disseminate information to everyone all at once.
Information that trickles out becomes disinformation. Remember the telephone game? It's just like that. If people don't hear it from you, then they probably heard it wrong.

Conversations About Others

Avoid gossip.
In retail, we talk all day long. Retail is a business, and we need to figure out what's working and what's not.

Inevitably the leaders in the building will end up talking about the other people on the team. When the conversation turns to the staff, it needs to be positive or constructive and done out of earshot of other employees.

Avoid gossip as much as you can. People on your team will gossip with each other; it's human nature. As a leader in the building, stay out of it. If an associate comes to you with a problem with another associate who was hurtful or disrespectful, that's different. Then you need to get involved and possibly partner with HR. But if it's simply gossip about another person, I don't want to know about it.

If you talk poorly of people when they're not around, your team will lose trust in you. If you talk badly about other people, they assume you'll talk badly about them too.

When team members come up in conversation, it should be positive.

"She's so cool."
"Her jeans looked so cute today! Did you see them?"
"He handled that customer so well!"
"They helped me with the denim wall. Doesn't it look
good?"

Positivity breeds positivity.

Similarly, don't talk to a leader about another leader's struggles. That conversation should stay between the two of you. As you set the stage for respect and positivity, it will grow. When gossip pops up around you, make it clear that you're not going to participate, and the team will get the message.

Be Fair

Justice is quite powerful, and it was important to me when I led teams. I understood that, as a Store Manager, I have a role in the store. My role is important, but I am not better than anyone else because of my title. I do not get special treatment because I am at the leadership team's top. I embraced leadership like, "Hey! I'm going on this crazy adventure. Want to come along, learn some stuff, and help me out?"

Specific job requirements sometimes meant I left my store early to help another store. Sometimes I had to walk the mall to recruit. Other days were spent at manager meetings or helping with floor moves. Whatever. All of these things were unique to my position. They didn't make me special.

Kermit the Frog wasn't the star of *The Muppet Show*. He made everything work and let others into the spotlight. Conversely, Miss Piggy was self-involved and liked to hog the limelight. You see the difference. Be Kermit.

Each leader on your team will have a unique skill set. Meet them where they are and help them learn what they don't know yet.
Be fair with things like these:
- Ensure every manager has a weekend off—including yourself.
- Honor requests as much as the business will allow.
- Don't be cranky when people ask for time off —encourage it.
- When you approve a request, don't schedule that person to close every day for a week as a punishment for taking time off. (I've heard

this happens often, and it's not cool.)

There will never be a good time for the Store Manager to be out of the business. With that being said, October and April are usually good months to be gone as long as you're not gone during spring break (if that affects your business).

Plan your vacations for the year now. Get the time off approved; then, you can figure out if you want to go somewhere. No one will do this for you, and it's essential. Now you see your time blocked off, and you get to look forward to it.

When someone else makes a request, you won't feel bitter about it because your vacation is coming. Leaders who understand that they are not the star of the show develop teams that work together. Be fair, approve time off, and encourage people to thrive outside this job.

Request time off for yourself now. Grant weekends off. Listen to the needs of your team members, and work with them. Be Kermit, not Miss Piggy (no shade, MP).

Corrective Action

Managing people is usually challenging, and every day is different.

Humans are complex, and we all have unique backgrounds and life experiences that make us who we are. That's great, but it can sometimes lead to confusion or mixed emotions. Sometimes you will have to deliver a write-up or have an uncomfortable conversation with someone on your team. Yes, this is the crummy part of the job, but you can tilt the conversation, so it's encouraging.

People don't want to suck.
Know that most people want to come to work and do a good job. People likely are not plotting to go in and mess up. Most mistakes come from a misunderstanding or miscalculations.

I will use tardiness as an example because it's clear-cut. I followed a coaching process that goes like this:

First, coach in the moment—
"Hey, Marcie, you're ten minutes late. What happened? I was worried about you."

Marcie: "There was a traffic jam."

"Okay, I get you. Yeah, traffic is bad this time of day. I always leave fifteen minutes earlier at this time of day. Is it possible for you to leave earlier?"

Marcie will probably say yes and agree to be on time for her next shift.

The next time it happens, talk with her in the back room. This conversation will be more serious in tone, and you'll let her know that the next time she's late, you'll be moving to a write-up.

"Hey Marcie, come chat with me in the office when you get your stuff put away."

Marcie will stop in, probably nervous.

You can say: "I know we've talked about you getting here on time, and I know you're trying. Is there anything you need from me to help you out? Should I schedule you later?"

Listen and hear her out. Repeat back anything that needs verification.

"Okay, great, so you don't need me to schedule you later, and you're going to stop studying ten minutes earlier so you can get here. Awesome. I know you can do it. Just so you know, the next time you're late, we will move to a write-up. But I don't think we'll need to because I know you can do it. Thanks for letting me know what you were struggling with."

If she's late again, you will move to a write-up where you'd both sign the documentation. One more time, and she's eligible to go to a final written warning. Typically when someone has three violations for the same policy violation, you can potentially let them go. Partner with HR. The next time they're late, they may be eligible for termination after the final written warning.

I didn't have to fire too many people throughout my career, but when I did, they always knew it was coming. It wasn't a surprise. I got to know my HR specialist well. I called her with all kinds of quirky questions. I spent most of my career in California, and labor laws are stringent. I often needed someone to guide me through the best way to handle unique situations.

How to have difficult conversations -

When you approach difficult conversations in a real way, they're much more manageable. Take your "boss" label off for a minute and talk to the person like a human. Everyone is different, and you can show up for them in a way they'll understand.

"Can I have a difficult conversation with you?" is a great opener. Now the person knows this conversation is serious, and they're ready to listen.

One holiday season, I wrote someone up for returning something from online that they weren't supposed to return. I wouldn't usually write someone up for that; it would be more of a conversation like, "Hey Tony, look alive; we aren't supposed to return this."

But this time, I'd had it. The associate had been messing up for two weeks straight. He was tenured, so he knew the job well; he was just being careless, and I was frustrated.

We sat down in the office.

"Look, man, for the past two weeks working with you has been a challenge. You wander off, you talk too much, and you need to recover your zone better.

Yesterday, you returned this item from online that you weren't supposed to. We're all tired, and we need your help. I know you're capable of way more than what you're showing us, so can you step it up?"
He admitted he'd been slacking and listened to me. He signed his write-up and stepped up for the rest of the season.

Addressing behavior issues or writing people up can be a drag. You have to devote the time that you don't feel like you have to this; really, you're just hoping the problem corrects itself. But in reality, it won't. No problem ever went away magically. I had to address it. Have the conversation and set clear expectations so you can move forward.

Share Credit. Collaborate.

Plagiarism feels rampant in the world of online writing. I've had my words stolen more than once. It's too easy to copy/paste words and try to pass them off as your own. But, it must feel gross for the thief. Who knows, maybe not.

Whenever I've confronted people, they would remove my messages and not respond, proudly leaving my words under their names. The audacity. When people do this in the work world, others notice quickly.

This is obvious advice, but don't steal other people's ideas. When you give credit where credit is due, you look super cool. Intelligent people understand that giving credit to the person who had the idea first comes across as a boss move. It makes you look humble, supportive, and confident.

Self-assured leaders understand that great ideas come from everywhere and everyone. Collaboration is one of the most fun aspects of running a team. Becoming an idea magnet pushes people to places they didn't know they could go.

Reminder: Your store is not yours. It belongs to the entire team. One of the most powerful sentences you can ask your team is, "What do you think?" When you encourage everyone to come to the table and create solutions, your team understands that you value them and see them as equals.

When you're talking to your boss about what's going on in the store, use the following language:
"We did this." (not "I")
"We worked on…"
"We partnered on…."
"Katie helped me with that."
"Elizabeth figured out how to flip this and make it work better."

When I ran teams, I couldn't wait to tell my boss about someone else's great idea. Why? Because I was so proud of them, and I couldn't wait to share their ideas with the world.

If you've ever had someone take your ideas, you

know how awful it feels, especially when someone is supposed to be helping you, like your boss. Similarly, I have a friend whose boss told him, "I've already thought of everything. None of your ideas are new." Guess what? He never tried to partner with that boss again, even when he had great ideas.

Bosses who steal ideas or shut out collaboration create uncertainty within their teams and mistrust. When your concept is snatched, it causes you to shut down and not share so quickly in the future. Idea theft causes division and gossip. It rips the cohesive fabric at the seams. There is no upside to taking ideas from others and sharing them as your own. There is no upside to telling your team that you know everything and their thoughts are useless to you.

When you give credit to the person who had the idea, it's all upside. There's no downside to saying, "Eric thought of this!" There's no downside to saying, "Thanks for your insight. I'll think about it." Champion others without fail. There is no downside. You'll always win.

When you promote the work of others, you'll create a team of hardworking people who can't wait to come to work and contribute their talents. Your store is also your team's store. It belongs to everyone who works there. Whether it's someone's first day or they've been there for five years, the store belongs to everyone. Share it. Welcome ideas and partnerships. Share credit and collaboration. Your team will gel and thrive even when you're not in the building.

Set your leaders up for success: Look ahead and anticipate needs.
Protect the next shift. Set your next leader up for success. Plan ahead.

When I closed my store at night, I thought about what the opening manager would need the following day. After I counted the tills, walked the recovery, and partnered with the sales associates, I'd get the opening manager set up. I'd ensure the office and breakroom were clean. I'd leave any last notes. I'd stock the cash wrap—anything to make the next leader's job a little easier.

When I opened, I'd do the same thing. Before I left for the day, I'd help clean up the cash wrap or put hardware away. I'd ensure projects were cleaned up so the closers could have a smooth night. Before I left, I would find the closing manager and ask them, "Do you need anything from me before I leave?" We could discuss any last-minute details, and then I'd head out for the day. As I walked out, I'd say goodbye to each associate individually and thank them for their help.

"See you later, Emma. Do you work tomorrow? Awesome! See you then. Thanks for your help today."

That's a small interaction that builds a strong foundation for mutual respect. Do it every day and do it with sincerity.

Avoid Burnout

One thing thriving teams do well is support each other using insider language. Not corporate jargon. It's more like a natural language you'd share with a friend. A shorthand language is created as the work is done each day. Pretty soon, you're all using the words you've created to get the job done faster and more efficiently.

Some of it was regional, some of it was cultural, and some of it was because we were exhausted. We had more than one word to describe burnout in our store.

Burnout can sneak up on you in retail. You think working that seven-day stretch will be all right, but once you get to day five and realize you still have to work two more days, you start to get fried.

Walking through the front door can make you cranky. I'd tell my team, "I'm on day five of seven," and they'd know exactly what I meant. Then they'd lean in for support. We used to call burnout "burnt," "french fry," or "crispy." When you said, "I'm a french fry," everyone knew what that meant. It means you need a day off and may be a little slower than usual today. It meant your brain felt like scrambled eggs. We'd support each other extra hard that day.

There was no judgment behind this description.

We've all been there. We'd use this shorthand language to communicate and back each other. When my co-manager told me, "I think our DM is a little crispy," I knew what she was saying. It means she has too much on her plate, and her fuse is getting short. It meant not asking her for anything extra for the next few days.

Burnout is common in retail, and it will happen, but you can take some precautions.

- Ensure that you're not working more than five days straight.
  ○ Usually, I'd need a break after three days. Taking Thursday off was ideal because I'd need a day of quiet (a day of zero questions) after Monday, Tuesday, and Wednesday.

- Take one weekend off each month.
  ○ I was terrible at this, and I almost always worked Saturdays. However, getting two days off in a row once in a while will help combat burnout. Even if it's not a weekend, schedule two days off once in a while.

- Get a vacation scheduled now.
  ○ Ask your boss, put it on the calendar, and get it going. You can figure out where you're going later. If you don't, the year will fly by like a runaway train, and you'll wind up like a french fry.

- Be strategic about when you close and open.

○ The dreaded "clopen"—when you close and have to open the next day—is a burnout accelerator. This really takes a toll. You can do it once a week, but that's about it. Writing a well-planned schedule will help you avoid burnout and help your team prevent it. Consider all of the above for the people on your team, not just you. This way, you can support a smart work/life balance.

Support the health and rest of your team members, and they will stay invested. A day will come when you hit the wall and become totally fried. It happens to all of us. It's okay. Take care of yourself. Schedule a day off where you do nothing, if at all possible. Yes, you'll have to do your typical house and family activities, but don't make appointments, don't schedule a coffee date, just rest. Use that time to heal and let your nervous system come down. This will help you stay well.

Even when you do everything right, burnout can still occur. Take care of yourself and your team, and you will make it to the other side.

How To Handle Bad Days

Not every store visit I ever had went well. Many of them never happened at all; my Regional Manager at one company canceled every visit he ever scheduled with me. I was largely left to fend for myself.

Much of the feedback I received early on in my career was harsh. There was no hand-holding; I had to listen, implement, and move on. If you've ever seen the movie, *A League of Their Own*, you may recall the famous "There's no crying in baseball" scene. Retail is like that. There's no crying in retail.

That's how I came up, anyway. The industry is changing, but surviving often takes grit. A bad day can hit you when you least expect it. Your boss will be extra harsh. A customer will yell at you. All your closers will call out. First thing first, breathe. Take a deep breath.

Listen to your boss's direction, and adjust based on her feedback. Do whatever you can to get that angry customer out of your store. Hopefully, they leave happy, but it's also not okay for them to yell at you. You can request to be treated with respect before you help them.

Next, call for backup. If someone calls out, your priority needs to be filling that shift if you can. Keep a list of associates who may want more hours and contact them first.

Lastly, remember, this is only ONE day of your life. Tomorrow will be different. Tell your customers when something goes sideways. Be upfront. They'll have patience.

Get through it. Go home, take a shower, drink water, and get some sleep. Scream in your car, or cry your eyes out. Move through the emotions in whatever way works for you as long as you are not hurting other living creatures or yourself. Do what you can to get through it.

Take more deep breaths. You'll be okay.

How To Manage Up. Building Relationships With Bosses.

How many times have you received an email from your boss, and you could tell she was frustrated? There was excessive use of capitalization; an overabundance of exclamation points. After you read that email, you probably thought, "Well, today is not the day to ask for anything extra." You'd be right. You'd also understand how to manage up successfully.

Make your boss's job easier.
That's what's at the heart of managing up—making your boss's job easier—but there's more to it. Managing up requires a slew of soft skills that most likely aren't taught. You have to pay attention to tiny details and understand the nuances of how your boss works.

I was never taught how to manage up. I had never heard that language, but I understood that my boss was busy, and if I could make her job easier, it would be better for the entire district. If you know how to read a room, you're good at managing up.

The Soft Skills/Emotional Quotient/People Skills

I'm not a fan of the term "soft skills". "EQ" or "people skills" seems to track more accurately in my mind. But they all mean essentially the same thing.

Teaching someone how to read a room can be challenging. There's no step-by-step guide. There are no hard and fast rules. The same is true for managing up. The most important thing is to pay attention and observe. Is your boss a morning person? Does she thrive on Mondays, or is she typically overwhelmed that day? Does she prefer short, quick email responses, or does she like deeper explanations?

Everyone has a different work style, so pay attention to these small details and look for patterns. Soon, you'll understand the best time to reach her and catch her when she may have fewer distractions. Also, understand that she is a human trying to do her best, just like you.

Managing up means relationship building with your bosses. It doesn't mean that you should walk on eggshells around your bosses or that you need to be the leader in this relationship.

Store visits

I typically had good store visits because I kept my store clean and ran my store the way the company wanted, but I also understood how to manage up.

When leaders from the corporate office stopped by, I knew how to mix small talk with business. I watched for nonverbal cues and sprang into action if anything was amiss. I didn't make excuses; I got to work. When visits were great, we had more time for conversation, and I listened intently to what was important in my leaders' lives. I followed up on those things the next time I saw them.

I listened more than I talked. I picked up an extraordinary amount by observation.

Managing up isn't schmoozing.
The most important thing here is that this wasn't calculated. I didn't do it to position myself as a favorite or to be liked. I genuinely cared about what was important to my leaders and wanted to learn more about the business.

I'm honestly a terrible schmoozer. Managing up is different from schmoozing. It's creating a partnership with your boss and corporate partners so you can all move forward as a team. You all have the same goal, make it work together.

You can advocate for your team more effectively when you manage up well. Your boss may be more open to hearing about how great Toni is, even though her first impression wasn't great. Keep it sincere.

I've been on the receiving end of someone trying to

manage up with me as their leader, but it wasn't a genuine attempt. They wanted to flatter me and stroke my ego, but I called them on it and told them it wasn't necessary. When it's calculated, it's obvious and makes me feel gross.

Managing up is a critical leadership skill.
Get to know your leaders and learn how you can support their work. Communicate and connect genuinely; you'll learn more about the company, and you may get an inside look at what your leaders do. It's beneficial for you—you can test the waters and see if you want to move up. It's also helpful for your boss—they get a more impactful partnership from one of the people they lead.

Now, when you see an email come through with a celebratory tone...quick, shoot your vacation request over asap! Timing is everything, friends. That's managing up.

Tips For Leveling Up

Sometimes store standards can slip. Leaders are gone on vacation, you have a heavy shipment week, maybe you have newer leaders, whatever, it happens.

Post a recovery scorecard in the back room if you start to notice that the recovery at closing hasn't been up to standard. We used a whiteboard. Make it easy and use a scale from one to five. One is terrible, and five is excellent. A passing score is a three.

The closing manager divides the store into recovery sections and makes notes on the zone chart regarding who is in charge of what.

Jenny: Women's dept.
Trey: Kid's dept.
Etc.

I did this when I had newer leaders who were still developing. It taught them what to look for as they walked the floor at closing. It also makes the store recovery a team effort.

The opening manager or merchandiser would walk

the floor and score the closing efforts in the morning. Each department would get a score, as would the overall recovery. They would also note anything that looked exceptional (Wow! Denim wall!) and anything that had been missed (The impulse carts could use some love).

The closing scorecard will help your team correct areas of the store that are typically missed. A dirty cash wrap and messy folding carts are usual culprits.

Again, keep all written communication slanted toward positive. Even if there was an area that was a total miss, like clearance, you can leave a note on the board like, "Looks like we forgot to recover clearance - oh no!" That way it translates like "oops" rather than "you suck."

How to ace your next corporate visit -
There it is. The date on the calendar is highlighted in your office: The Visit

This means a group of people (who most definitely use a dry cleaning service regularly) will descend on your store and walk around to observe what's happening.
These people may or may not have ever worked a retail floor, but nevertheless, they're going to walk around in a cluster and take a keen look for any mistakes.

You've alerted your leaders and your sales staff.

You've instructed them all to be "visit ready," which means:
- In dress code
- On time
- Not hungover

The truth is that you will be called out for something. It's why they came. Even if your store is flawless, they'll give you a goal to work toward. No matter how much you've prepared, you'll be dinged on some misstep. It's fine.

The fresh-dressed,dry cleaning crew wants to hear how you respond to criticism. You need to listen to it and tell them how you'll proceed. You must avoid saying:
"That wasn't me."
"I didn't know."
"It was like that when I got here."

It doesn't matter. If it's your store, it's your problem. When you assign blame, it comes across as insecurity. When you accept responsibility and tell them what action you will take to fix it, they'll understand that you're the right person for the job, and the mood will stay lighthearted. If you're operationally sound, and your team knows what's expected, you're already on your way to a good visit.

There is one thing you cannot talk your way of: a dirty store. Make sure you've cleaned everything at least twice. Double-check:
- Your office

- The bathroom
- Folding carts
- Dusty fixtures

On visit days, the entire team kept a Swiffer in our pockets, and we'd dust all day.

If you've gotten overwhelmed by the workload and neglected the essential cleanliness of the store, you're in trouble. Anything else can be negotiated and should be left as-is so the suits can get an accurate idea of your struggles. Was the shipment too heavy this week? Is your buy-online-pickup-in-store system adequate, or is it causing you grief? They need to know the true answer so they don't pile more work on you, thinking you're all good.

Store visits are nerve-wracking no matter what you do. Know your numbers. Know how your store is doing versus your comp numbers. Clean your store well, and inform the staff of the visit date. Everything else is up to chance and the mood of your visitors. Do what you always do: show up, do your best, and involve the whole team. Your leadership skills will translate. The suits know that you're all working hard.

How to lead a sales floor with 15 + associates -
Leading a sales floor successfully takes a complex skill set. You must be totally present in the moment, but you must also be an hour ahead of yourself.

Ron Thurston, the author of *Retail Pride*, dedicates

a whole section in his book to focus. He describes focus as "Watching the finish line as you watch the hour."

I love that description because it gets to the heart of what we do when we run the floor. It is challenging to describe, but that quote is one of the best I've ever read.

When you run a sales floor, you need to know the following:
- The sales goal for the day and the hour (and the week, quarter, and year)
- Who is currently shopping in the store
- Which associates are in charge of which zones
- What time your associates are off
- What time they need to take their breaks
- Who is coming in next

Walk figure 8's around the floor so you can check in with everyone, see where customers are, and help sales associates if they need it. You can also greet people and watch for sketchy behavior.

Go-backs are an easy task to complete while running the floor because you're still moving around and you have your head up. The last thing you want to do as the manager in charge is fold down a table. You'll get lost in it and never look up. (I know you think you won't. You will. It's happened to me countless times.)

When I was first learning to run larger teams on the floor, I kept the zone chart with me to keep track of all the breaks. I avoided using a clipboard because it was bulky and awkward, and I wanted to be able to move faster.

The more you can zone your staff at the beginning of the hour, the more successful you'll be. If you have enough people to schedule someone to answer the phone, it's a lifesaver. That person could be doing go-backs and listening for the phone ringing. That way, you don't have four people running to grab a phone call.

For years, I kept a pen stuck through my ponytail. I'd write everything on that zone chart. I'd check off breaks and lunches, write recovery notes, and write reminders for the next day. When you're running a sales floor, you can seldom leave it. Your eyes need to be everywhere at once.

Going to the back to write a note or to send an email is next to impossible. An Assistant Manager I led used to write names and break times on her hand when she was learning. Hey, whatever works. Your situational awareness here is everything, and you'll get better as you practice it.

Running the floor with two leaders: Operations and Selling -
If you're fortunate enough to have two leaders on the floor, decide who will be the Operations Manager

and who will be Selling. I often used this setup on weekends, and it works great.

The Operations Manager will...
- help the cashiers
- answer the phone if someone calls asking for a manager
- check in associates/check out associates
- get the deposit for the armored guard
- conduct bag checks
- etc.

The Selling Manager will...
- team sell with the associates
- dish out product knowledge
- work the fitting rooms with an associate
- bring additional items to the fitting rooms
- set a positive tone throughout the sales floor
- be on hand to answer questions from the selling team on the floor

Be sure to tell your team which leader is doing what so they know whom to go to with questions.

Whenever I worked with my co-manager, Thao, and the associates didn't know who was in charge of what that day, we became "KitThao." Literally, the associates would say both of our names together. It became a running joke.

Eliminate confusion, and be clear about what each leader is doing.

Evaluations And Self-Evaluations

Yearly evaluations are always a blessing and a curse. Feedback is essential, but you never feel like you have time to write them. Carve out a few hours off the floor and write your self-evaluation and your leaders 'reviews.

The self-eval
Take your time. Think back over the past year.
- Whom did you hire that was awesome?
- Whom did you promote?
- Whom did you develop?
- Did you work any stretch assignments?
- Did you lead meetings?
- Did you take a risk and it worked?
- Did it not work?
- What did you learn?

Steer clear of sentences that begin with "I think." We know "you think," you're writing it. Stick to declarative statements.

"I'm a resource for the district."
"I lead from the front."
"All hiring goals were met."
"Conflict makes me uncomfortable. I'd like to get better at having coaching conversations."

Write it, and then revisit it. You may want to add to it or change it a little. Just start. Beginning is the hardest part. Once you get going and start reflecting, you'll be able to power through.

Review your leaders.
Your leaders should get evaluations similarly to how you write your self-eval. Statements should be declarative and not revolve around feelings. Stick to facts.

"Allegra is punctual."
"Iliana learns and implements quickly."
"Amanda does not follow through with delivering corrective action."

When you sit down to deliver these reviews, keep in mind that what you're telling them should not be a surprise. At the end of every review, I would ask, "Was any of this a surprise, or was it what you thought it would be?" They would usually say it wasn't a surprise or it was better than they thought. Evaluations can be scary.

Conversations about development should be happening regularly. When you tell Amanda that she hasn't followed through with delivering corrective action, she should be nodding her head and saying, "Yes, I know. That's true." No review should leave the employee blindsided.

I've been blindsided in a review more than once, and it is beyond confusing. I couldn't figure out why my boss didn't address her concerns with me before we sat down for this annual evaluation. I still don't know. I'm guessing it was poor planning or fear on her part. Perhaps she didn't know how to give constructive criticism. Either way, it was sucky. Keep open and honest feedback going all year and you'll avoid the awkward conversations during review time.

PRIDE

Retail leaders carry so much pride with them...and grit. It never ceases to amaze me. They treat their stores like their personal business. Working early mornings and long nights, they'll do whatever's necessary to make the business successful. This was never more clear to me than when my store came out of a complete remodel.

In 2015, we were the first store in our district to get a full remodel. It was thrilling. It was also one of the most challenging projects I've ever worked on. The store was open during the remodel, so a plywood wall was built through the middle of the store. We had two plywood fitting rooms and a makeshift shoe room because we carried so many shoes. Our back room would not hold them all.

The noise was constant, and we had to field customer questions about the construction and be in continuous contact with our DM, corporate advisors, and the construction crews. Keep in mind that our store was comping (beating last year's sales numbers) throughout the entire remodel, which is total insanity. It was busy.

We worked three overnight shifts to accommodate

the construction. One night to move everything to one side of the store, transfer out merchandise, and install the plywood divider. One night to flip all the product to the other side. And one night to set up for our reopening and to tear down the plywood wall. Each of my overnight shifts turned out to be about fourteen hours. I'd work from 8 pm to 10 am.

A project of this size took help from not only our district but our entire region. Massive amounts of people turned up for each overnight shift and worked tirelessly to make this remodel a reality. Some moved hardware, folded denim walls, and put new tables together. The visual team worked miracles merchandising our new walls.

One spring weekend during the remodel, it got hot. Really hot. We had no air conditioning, but no one told us about it. We had no idea we wouldn't have AC. We were still supposed to be in the winter dress code, and the team was absolutely dying all layered up. I told them to switch to the summer dress code and wear whatever they needed to in order to stay cool. Shorts, T-shirts, whatever. (Remember, bend, don't break. I wasn't about to call anyone for approval; I was going to take care of my team.)

Customers shopped quickly and expressed sympathy for us on their way out of the store. We wiped the sweat off our faces with paper towels. We took a lot of water breaks, and we made it into the following week when we got our AC back.

Every day in a complete remodel is a gigantic new adventure.

When our grand opening day came, we opened the doors to a beautiful, modern, gorgeously merchandised new building that even had a wall full of skateboards. I walked through the building, and my emotions caught me off guard. An enormous sense of pride welled up in me; I had to fight back tears. We had done it. All the long hours, overnights, and sweat had paid off. All that grit and determination had paid off.

Looking around at all the faces of the people on my team, I could tell they were all beaming. Our joy was palpable, and it spilled over.

YOU GOT THIS

As you navigate your retail career, you will have super-hard days with tons of work. You'll get exhausted, you'll get fed up, and then you'll finish a project with your team and realize that it was all worth it. You'll all be totally crispy and laugh hysterically at something together because you're all fried.

Retail will teach you skills you never thought you could learn. You'll become more resourceful than you ever thought possible, and you'll become the reason that someone wanted to come to work today.

Leading a team is an honor. Put people on your team first, and you'll always make the right decision.

I'm cheering you on,
Kit

A HEARTFELT
THANK YOU TO:

Matthew Campoy, my husband. He has stood by my side through all my crazy ideas and said, "DO IT." Your unwavering support is like an Arizona sunrise. Let's grab our backpacks and head out somewhere.

Natascha Bock & Michelle Ocampo, my two best friends from high school. We still laugh like we're sixteen years old when we get together. I still see these amazing women every year, and it was Michelle who said to me, "You should really write a book." And I believed her.

Thao Dao & James Garcia, our group text thread will never die. I worked with these two phenomenal humans at my last store for at least six years. The three of us got through the COVID closure together and so much more. Thao, thank you for being one of the first people to read this book. James, thank you for the design input. I'll see you in yoga.

Cindy Davis, one of my best friends whom I met in retail. She can now officially read my mind and is a total badass. I feel invincible with her by my side. Thanks for helping me keep my head on straight.

Carole Marlowe, my mom. She reads absolutely everything I write, even the Web3 articles that she doesn't necessarily care about. She's been my hype-woman from day one, and she let me read advanced novels at a young age. Thank you.

Carissa May, another fantastic retail friend. Thank you for following me to work for different companies and being so amazing to work with. Thank you for being among the first to read this book and for all the coffee and margaritas.

Danielle Neal - she and I stepped up and ran a store together (for like six months!) when we had no store manager or visual manager. I ran operations and she ran hiring and training. We smashed it. We've been friends ever since.

Zane Stanley—You applied to work in my store on Halloween dressed as a giraffe. I knew it would be a fit. Thank you for your years of hard work, friendship, and savvy design skills. You're the best.

Marty Thomas, my dad. He has an extensive leadership background in the military and business. Thanks for all the leadership discussions over scoops of Häagen-Dazs® ice cream. Cheers!

Pat Thomas, my stepmom. She reads more than anyone I know. She would read a book while she listened to an audiobook at the same time if she could. Thank you for sharing your love of books, history, and travel with me.

Ryan Thomas, my brother. He knows about all the things I do not. Thanks for dragging me around in a wagon as a child through dirt piles to "toughen me up." It worked. Thanks for betting on me.

Jackson—Yes, Jackson is our dog. His messy fur, underbite, and independent attitude make him the best dog ever. Thanks for getting me up and out the door every morning, dude.

The LinkedIn Community, you know who you are. Thank you for being so actively involved in the creation of this book. You helped me with everything along the way, from the outline to the book cover. Thank you for all your input. This book would not exist without your help.

Special shoutout to a few more amazing people:

Carmen Ballesteros, Eric Brozgold, Kelly Eden, Heather Fenwick, Ash Jurberg. Max Klein, Tom Kuegler, Katina Lindsey, Michelle Maze, Duncan Molloy, Roi Perets, Ron Thurston, and Evan Wildstein.

Thank you to every single one of my family and friends.

I Love Ya!

ONE LAST THING...

Thank you so much for reading this book. I poured a lot of heart, soul, and coffee into it.

Could you do me a favor? Please review this book on Amazon. Whether you thought it was stellar, a total bummer, or anywhere in between, I'd love to have your feedback.

Reviews are the best way for an author like me to get discovered. Readers like you can help make it happen.

Thanks in advance.

Stay rad,

Kit

ABOUT THE AUTHOR

Kit Campoy has been called The Voice of the Frontline by the readers of her online content.

In 2021, Kit began sharing leadership tips and motivational messages to the retail community on LinkedIn daily. She often ended her posts with a "you got this" nudge of encouragement. Before long, her LinkedIn audience began asking her to write a book of her best practices.

Kit is honored to give back to the retail community she called home for over two decades.

Although Kit achieved a B.S. in merchandising, her true education came from leading frontline retail teams. In 2022, she stepped away from her retail career to pursue writing full-time.

Kit hails from Tucson, Arizona, and lives in Southern California with her husband. When she's not writing with her dog by her side, Kit spends her time reading, road-tripping, and sipping iced coffee. She's cheering you on every step of the way in your leadership journey.

Join Kit in her leadership training and advocacy of frontline associates.

Kit Campoy

Editor: Alicia Rust

Cover design: Kit Campoy

Cover formatted by: 100 covers dot com